I.S.B.N. 0 85079 162 6

SUNDAY EXPRESS & DAILY EXPRESS
CARTOONS

Fortieth Series

AN EXPRESS BOOKS PUBLICATION

© 1986 Express Newspapers p.l.c., Fleet Street, London, EC4P 4JT
Printed in Great Britain by Purnell Book Production Limited. Member of The BPCC Group

U·K £2·10

FOREWORD

by

BOBBY
ROBSON

National Coach/

England Team Manager

The first requirement for survival as a football manager is undoubtedly a sense of humour. In a profession where the one sure thing is the applicability of Murphy's Law that whatever can go wrong will, he who laughs not lasts not.

The ability to extract humour from unpromising situations is priceless and, as far as I am concerned, there is no-one in the world better at this than Giles. His characters are fallible and prone to error — just like footballers (and their managers). They are also very funny.

Giles' talent and the reason for his perennial popularity is that he makes us laugh with them and not at them. His cartoons are full of affection, totally devoid of malice and meticulous down to the minutest detail.

Giles, if you're ever in need of a job, I think you'd make a great manager.

Bobby Robson.

"The MCC ordered it . . . keep you fellas from running on the pitch, pinching the stumps."

Daily Express, June 20th, 1985

"*You* may not think it's very nice weather for camping — your son Tristan thinks it's great."

Sunday Express, June 23rd, 1985

"He's got very nice manners — every time he steals a strawberry he says 'Thanks, doll'."

Daily Express, June 25th, 1985

"Ladies and Gentlemen, until tennis is resumed we have a 15-round umpires' challenge contest."

Daily Express, June 27th, 1985

"Pippa! Would you please ask your husband not to phone while our Chief is making her anniversary speech."

Sunday Express, June 30th, 1985

"What kept you — the traffic hold-up on the M1?"

Daily Express, July 2nd, 1985

"He opened his window and shouted: 'You're sucking a Polo Mint! OUT!'"

(Headline: Man ordered out of taxi because he was smoking)

Daily Express, July 4th, 1985

"I'd like to see a woman vicar in a dog-collar get me to a church — beg pardon, your Reverence."

Sunday Express, July 7th, 1985

"Thank your darling daughter for blurting it all over the place she'd got a Boris Becker autograph."

Daily Express, July 9th, 1985

"Simply riding your boy round Oxford on a tandem won't make him an Einstein, sir."

(Headline: A father insists on attending University with young degree-winning daughter)

Daily Express, July 11th, 1985

"The children are back — they've videoed the whole sixteen hours of yesterday's Rock Concert
in case you missed it."

Sunday Express, July 14th, 1985

"Apart from Idi Amin being kicked out of Queen's Tennis Club and McEnroe taking over Uganda, anything else happen while we were away?"

Daily Express, July 30th, 1985

"Frankie's not very happy — they've written on his card 'Refer to Natural History Museum'."

Daily Express, August 1st, 1985

"Stop telling me the Queen Mother is twice my age and does her own garden and you bet it doesn't look a mess like ours."

Sunday Express, August 4th, 1985

"You'll never believe it, darling — I've searched every street in the City and not a berry in sight."

Daily Express, August 6th, 1985

"Thank the TV strike — missing your mooring and slipping into the Solent didn't make News At Ten."

Daily Express, August 8th, 1985

"You must make allowances for them getting bored with non-stop rain and Scrabble."

Sunday Express, August 11th, 1985

"Stop arguing, Grandma, you know her rules — everybody out immediately after breakfast."

Daily Express, August 13th, 1985

"His first call — instruct his solicitors to sue the weathermen if it rains at Edgbaston, then sue BR if they get him there late."

Daily Express, August 15th, 1985

"Golf is out, Vic, thanks to that clever judge and his 'Women are the weaker sex'."

Sunday Express, August 18th, 1985

"You're one of 'em who say we only need one-man trains — put your bike on yourself, mate."

Daily Express, August 22nd, 1985

"The Skipper's not coming — too wet. He's left the food on board and instructions if you'd like to take her on your own."

Sunday Express, August 25th, 1985

"Who put this in the local shop window? 'For sale — Two unruly parents obsessed with tidying up'."

Daily Express, August 27th, 1985

"Mrs Cholmondeley-Smythe tells me you've been queuing all afternoon for tickets for this sizzling sex-pot Madonna film."

Daily Express, August 29th, 1985

"Here comes Rambo with the ices."

Sunday Express, September 1st, 1985

"Never seen churches doing such business on a weekday. It'll be these thanksgiving services for the children going back to school."

Daily Express, September 3rd, 1985

"The benefits of Mrs Thatcher's new Cabinet have not reached the public yet, Madam, embrocation and liver pills are the same price as yesterday."

Daily Express, September 5th, 1985

"I never want a drink when I go to football, it's after watching our lot play that I want one."

Sunday Express, September 8th, 1985

"If this emergency is for another pair of oafs going treasure hunting in a six-foot plastic boat,
I'm chucking 'em back!"

Daily Express, September 10th, 1985

"On guard, girls! Inside every one of 'em is a potential Harvey Smith."

Sunday Express, September 15th, 1985

"Mr Gorbachev? I've lost count — is it us to you or you to us today?"

Daily Express, September 17th, 1985

"How come we only got two spies for dad on the Exchange Market and Ivanovich's dad made 25?"

Daily Express, September 19th, 1985

"Hold it! Before we go in — Mr Burrows complains that 6 marrows, 5 lbs of tomatoes, and 2 doz. cauliflowers are missing from his shop."

Sunday Express, September 22nd, 1985

"The fact that your mother helped wash-up at a fete attended by Queen Victoria hardly qualifies you to write 12 volumes on the lives of the entire Royal Family."

Daily Express, September 24th, 1985

"Here he comes, moaning all the year about too wet to get the harvest in —
a couple of weeks' sun and it's too hard to plough for next year's harvest."

Daily Express, October 1st, 1985

"Grandma on politics . . . she'd give Hurricane Higgins 14 rounds in the ring with Frank Bruno, then send them both up to Liverpool to give Derek Hatton a hammering."

Daily Express, October 3rd, 1985

"I'm getting just a teeny bit fed up with her — Over here! I've found another one!"

Sunday Express, October 6th, 1985

"Excuse me, luv — there's a little microphone sticking on the back of your neck."

Daily Express, October 8th, 1985

"Teacher says behind every man there was a successful woman — like Nell Gwynne, Lady Hamilton, Lily Langtry, for starters."

Daily Express, October 10th, 1985

"That wasn't from Bergerac — I think Wills got that one from Alf Garnett."

(Headline: There were complaints about Prince Wills being allowed to watch the TV series Bergerac)

"I would urge that any bottle with a hammer & sickle label should be served to his Lordship with utmost caution."

Daily Express, October 15th, 1985

"These spectacles you say the Government says I am under obligation to replace —
I see they are dated October 1928."

Daily Express, October 17th, 1985

"The Queen's guests kept her waiting an hour and a quarter for dinner, but she didn't go out and leave silly notes like 'Your dinner's in the cat!' "

Sunday Express, October 20th, 1985

"It says: Canteen food can seriously damage your health. Telling that to our Florrie could seriously damage your health."

Daily Express, October 22nd, 1985

"The card from your sister in Llangollen should stand a chance, with one snag — it's whether it's in the first truck or the last."

Daily Express, October 24th, 1985

"Who set that thing to go off at 2 a.m. to remind me I've got an extra hour's sleep?"

Sunday Express, October 27th, 1985

"When you shake hands remember she doesn't like being called 'Di' and she certainly won't like being called 'Sheila'."

Daily Express, October 29th, 1985

"That one doesn't need to dress up for Halloween."

Daily Express, October 31st, 1985

"Did you write to the TV people saying we'd play on TV for half the price of the 1st Division?"

Sunday Express, November 3rd, 1985

"Apart from trading without a licence to sell — I'm checking if bathwater can be sold on Sundays."

(Headline: Americans queue to buy Royal bathwater)

Sunday Express, November 10th, 1985

"Hello Herbie, I didn't know you were interested in following Halley's Comet."

Daily Express, November 12th, 1985

"That's a bit thick — sentencing him to stay after school and watch Miss World for punishment."

Daily Express, November 14th, 1985

"Since Mary Whitehouse said EastEnders was disgusting Richard's in there half an hour before it starts."

Sunday Express, November 17th, 1985

"He does that every time British Rail put their fares up."

Sunday Express, November 24th, 1985

"I only said, 'You wouldn't happen to be one of those Kissogram cops?'."

Daily Express, November 26th, 1985

"The hijackers on social security say one more omelette like that and they'll blow you and your kitchen from here to Beirut."

Daily Express, November 28th, 1985

"Last year the little dears did him up in his Christmas cave — this year he's going to be ready for them."

Sunday Express, December 1st, 1985

"If you exercise your right to dismiss the jury — the plaintiff confesses it was he who attacked you, and the Judge is in a good mood — we might just have a chance."

Daily Express, December 3rd, 1985

"Real nice, Wally. Too bad if the Prince doesn't visit our shop floor after all."

Daily Express, December 5th, 1985

"Christmas comes but once a year — another fort for me and another doll's cradle for you."

Sunday Express, December 8th, 1985

"I've got to report to the Store Manager — a customer's complained that when she asked if we'd got any Star War games I said, 'No we aint — try the States'."

Daily Express, December 10th, 1985

"Ladies, whatever your opinion of damages awarded to rape victims, you must stop shouting 'chauvinist pigs' at their Lordships."

Daily Express, December 12th, 1985

"Those Teddy bears you 'found' up here and put in Christie's sale were the twins' Christmas presents."

Sunday Express, December 15th, 1985

"Pity you didn't check before you ordered a kissogram girl — the boss has brought his wife with him."

Daily Express, December 17th, 1985

"Just what we need with all these drunk mice and robins with holly in their hats.
A BBC Chief inviting everyone to write and tell him about TV violence!"

Daily Express, December 19th, 1985

"I think they heard you say they'd make a better Bonnie & Clyde, Vicar."

Sunday Express, December 22nd, 1985

"He's never nipped anyone before — he probably thought you were going to mug him."

Daily Express, December 24th, 1985

"Why don't you take the aunts for a nice walk while we get the lunch?"

"Don't shove, Mary — I want to get back to work as much as you want me to!"

Daily Express, December 31st, 1985

"Your Dad's New Year resolution — jogging. He only got to the end of the road where the police found him in a 'distressed condition' — could you go and pick him up?"

Daily Express, January 2nd, 1986

"I only asked him to try his new uniform for school tomorrow and he suddenly remembered he's got a recurrence of an old dormant ailment."

Sunday Express, January 5th, 1986

"Hurricane Higgins got a black eye falling off a horse — I got mine when my wife saw me looking at THAT!"

Daily Express, January 7th, 1986

"We didn't get much sleep or anything else with those damned lights beamed on us all night."

Daily Express, January 9th, 1986

"Well, in view of everyone complaining about arming the police with fast machine guns . . ."

Sunday Express, January 12th, 1986

"What odds will we give her on Wogan to move into No. 10 and Heseltine to take over Dirty Den on TV?"

Daily Express, January 14th, 1986

"Michael, Leon, Westland, Sikorsky — I appreciate they were the first sounds she uttered,
but aren't they rather odd names to call a girl?"

Sunday Express, January 19th, 1986

"It'll be much more fun knowing your wife could hop over in three hours."

Daily Express, January 21st, 1986

"Grandma ordered the escort — wants to make sure her pools get posted."

Daily Express, January 23rd, 1986

"That's my Henry! Calling to ask Daddy for my hand in marriage and turns up in a Westland helicopter!"

Sunday Express, January 26th, 1986

"Dad, why do you always tell us if we don't do our homework we'll never get to the top?"

Daily Express, January 28th, 1986

"New technology won't get very far with you turning up half an hour late with one of your blooming colds."

Daily Express, January 30th, 1986

"I thought you said you knew Murdoch personally and we wouldn't have any trouble getting in."

Sunday Express, February 2nd, 1986

"She read Egon Ronay's report that it's fashionable to go out for a Continental breakfast, then she comes back and has a traditional English one as well."

Daily Express, February 4th, 1986

"I don't know what the Queen's moaning about. Forty five minutes delay and no restaurant service is norm on our line."

Daily Express, February 6th, 1986

"10 Downing Street say they will give Grandma a knighthood if she will lay off politics for five minutes
so we can have a nap."

Sunday Express, February 9th, 1986

"Tell Fu Man Chu in there if he doesn't soon show, his 'Year of the Tiger' is up."

Daily Express, February 11th, 1986

"Is your husband up? I'm his Valentine Kissogram girl."

Daily Express, February 13th, 1986

"You ought to be ashamed! Betting the vicar 50-1 he couldn't get the course cleared at Wolverhampton in time for racing on Monday."

Sunday Express, February 16th, 1986

"Do you have to let everyone know you're an electrician from Fort Wapping?"

Daily Express, February 18th, 1986

"I hear he's complained to British Leyland that he's not satisfied with his 1951 Land-Rover and demands a new one."

Daily Express, February 20th, 1986

"My heart bleeds for our poor cricketers losing out there in all that terrible sun."

Sunday Express, February 23rd, 1986

"I wouldn't travel nude on British rail in a heatwave with their heat full on."

Daily Express, February 27th, 1986

"She says she hasn't used her extra pension on a luxury holiday in the sun to be told she can't get cornflakes, eggs and bacon, marmalade and toast."

Sunday Express, March 2nd, 1986

"Gentlemen, may I introduce you to Chalkie's answer to beautiful nude Russian models like they give 'em at Eton."

Daily Express, March 4th, 1986

"First race for a month and you can't get him out of the stable because he's too fat!"

"So Daddy suggested you bought me a nice new electric drill for Mother's Day so
he can make me some shelves."

Sunday Express, March 9th, 1986

"When it's the Queen coming ashore in a rough sea, it's: 'You have to admire her courage'.
When it's us, it's: 'Hurry up you old fool, they'll be shut'."

Daily Express, March 11th, 1986

"I know why he's not answering — bloody Cheltenham!"

Daily Express, March 13th, 1986

"In the case of more than one applicant we take the highest offer — not cut the cards."

Sunday Express, March 16th, 1986

"The other news is that tea is still the top drink in Britain — how's your St. Patrick's Day hangover, Mike?"

Daily Express, March 18th, 1986

"My wife collects the extra petrol tax off me as they didn't put any extra on Scotch."

Sunday Express, March 23rd, 1986

"Easter eggs and chicks have gone way down hill since I was a boy."

Daily Express, March 27th, 1986

"Shame they can't move that fallen tree in front of the garden tool shed until after Easter."

Sunday Express, March 30th, 1986

"Good morning, girls — I trust your holiday has invigorated you and you're looking forward to the Spring Sales."

Daily Express, April 1st, 1986

"Women win the right to work until 65 — round here they let you work till you're 165 for free."

Daily Express, April 3rd, 1986

"Her horse fell at the first fence, our cricketers are a pain in her neck, so she's off to pastures new."

Sunday Express, April 6th, 1986

"Chalkie's new curriculum — every man a fast bowler by end of term."

Daily Express, April 8th, 1986

"I know Prince Philip and Princess Anne use words like that, but you're not sending this!"

Daily Express, April 10th, 1986

"Bang goes our Royal Wedding on TV — six more of 'em want their weddings on the same day as Fergie."

Sunday Express, April 13th, 1986

"It's not all bad having a U.S. Base next door — Uncle Jim and the Aunts have decided on Cornwall this year instead of staying with us."

Sunday Express, April 20th, 1986

"If I can walk in without anybody stopping me you can walk out and take us to the Zoo on Bank Holiday."

Sunday Express, May 4th, 1986

(Headline: Prison razed to the ground in riots)

"That's the encouragement I like — According to the weatherman the wind has changed again so I'm wasting my time putting them in."

Sunday Express, May 11th, 1986

"The application for your husband to join Bob Geldof's 'Run the World' race definitely came from this address."

Sunday Express, May 18th, 1986

"Who's a lucky boy then? Fingers, Dinger and Spider are running round Britain for Sports Aid and you're keeping 'em covered."

Daily Express, May 20th, 1986

"Pa! We've won Concorde for the day, a Rolls-Royce and an apartment in the Falls Road for five years."

Daily Express, May 22nd, 1986

"We're not running for Sport Aid or for the good of our health — we're running because she's niggly about her damn pay-rise."

Sunday Express, May 25th, 1986

"Up since five cutting sandwiches for a picnic — what's the betting they're all back for lunch?"

Daily Express, May 27th, 1986

"If I was Mrs Thatcher and had to choose between cleaning up the Middle East or cleaning up dirty Britain I'd choose the Middle East."

Daily Express, May 29th, 1986

"If there's one thing makes me anti-Establishment it's a farmer nudging me in the back when I want to go to sleep."

(Headline: Hippies taking over farms)

Sunday Express, June 1st, 1986

"That bloody thing can come down for a start."

Daily Express, June 3rd, 1986

"Heaven knows our game could do with a streaker, but I'm not sure Vicar's good lady wife is quite streaker material."

Sunday Express, June 8th, 1986

"Trust her to win both bets — right about Bob Geldof and right about Bobby Robson."

(Headline: Football World Cup time had broken out)

Daily Express, June 12th, 1986

"I AM NOT SHOUTING! I'm simply stating you're not taking me out for a Father's Day lunch in this!"

Sunday Express, June 15th, 1986

"What do you mean — 'On your feet, everyone or we'll be late for the game!' We arranged this picnic before we even knew they'd be playing."

"His wife's put up with two weeks all-night football on TV, but she's damned if she's going to have all-night boxing!"

Daily Express, June 24th, 1986